Birmingh
Inns and Pubs

on old picture postcards

John Marks

1. The 'Three Horse Shoes', Pershore Road, Stirchley, with the photograph also show-ing — nearest the camera — the old forge. The inn sold Davenports' Celebrated and Noted Bottled Ales and Stouts. Postcard published by The Midland View Co. about 1910.

Designed and Published by
Reflections of Bygone Age
Keyworth, Nottingham
1992

**Printed by
Adlard Print and Typesetting Services,
Ruddington, Notts.**

INTRODUCTION

In Kelly's Directory of Birmingham for 1908, there are approximately 870 public houses, 1500 beer retailers, 15 licensed hotels and 14 Temperance hotels — and this for a very much smaller city than the one we know today. To serve these premises there were 32 small breweries within the city boundary. These were necessary because with horse-drawn drays, deliveries could only be made within a very limited area. The only alternative was for the big companies to move supplies by rail to local stations from which horse-drawn drays could operate. With the coming of mechanical vehicles, though, deliveries could be made over larger distances; home brewing or local breweries became uneconomic, and amalgamations or take-overs eliminated them, gradually leaving the giant companies of today.

It was not until I closely examined the postcards featured in this book that I realised whisky and its brands were as freely advertised on the exterior of pubs as was the brew of ale.

In view of the large number of pubs that existed in Birmingham at the beginning of the century, it is surprisingly difficult to find postcards of them — especially close-up ones. This lack of availability has to some extent governed my choice of cards. However, I have tried to present a balanced view of the (then) old and new, large and small, close-ups and general views of them in the streets they served. Pubs have always been landmarks, and it is still common to use their names as directional indicators.

Picture Postcards were first published in Britain in 1894, but it was not until a decade later that they began to take off, when in 1902 the Post Office allowed a message to be written on the address side. This meant that the whole of one side was available for the picture and obviously gave more scope to publishers. Photographic viewcards became very popular, and the postcard became the most important way of communicating news or messages, in much the same way as the telephone is used today. The years up to 1914 were the 'Golden Age' of picture postcards, when millions of imaginative designs covering every subject under the sun were published by a host of national and local firms. There's hardly a village or hamlet that wasn't documented at that time by a postcard publisher, though sometimes the number of cards available was unrelated to the size of a community.

The cards in this booklet come from a variety of publishers, including local firms such as the Midland View Co., Thomas Lewis, and George Birch. These details are included in the caption where known. If no mention is made of publisher, it can be assumed that a card was issued anonymously. Messages on the reverse are sometimes included if they are thought to be relevant or interesting.

John Marks
March 1992

ISBN 0 946245 51 7

Front cover: The 'Roe Buck' Inn at 132 High Street, Erdington, photographed by George Grigg, whose studio was at 140 High Street. Benjamin Kelsey (who supplied the Home-Brewed Ales) was a brewer in Henry Street, Aston. Postcard published about 1910.

BROAD STREET.

BIRMINGHAM.

2. The 'Old Crown' Inn in Broad Street on the corner of King Edward's Place is notable as the place where Henry Mitchell began brewing before founding Mitchells & Butlers and moving to Cape Hill. Early card of c.1903 vintage.

3. The famous trademark of Mitchells & Butlers on an advertising card posted to Shirley on August 28th 1918 with the message *"We regret we have **no** grains to offer you"*.

New Street, Birmingham. View 2.   *Photo, J. J. Ward, Coventry.*

4. The 'Waterloo Bar' in New Street is featured on the left of this postcard by J.J. Ward of Coventry. Next to the Bar was the Society of Artists' premises with its portico.

THE WATERLOO BAR, New Street, Birmingham.
G. W. HARDY, Proprietor.   *FREE HOUSE.*   Telephone 04550.

5. The interior of the 'Waterloo Bar' dining room and bar. Proprietor at the time of this c.1912 postcard was G.W. Hardy.

6. The 'Wheatsheaf', on the corner of Bow and Windmill Streets just off the Horsefair. H.W. Byfield was the licensee at the time of this c.1910 photographic card.

7. A Mitchells & Butlers pub at 255 Dartmouth Street in 1908. Kelly's Directory lists the premises as a 'Beer Retailer' (William Smith) but unfortunately does not give the name of the inn. The rear cab belonged to Benjamin Thorpe, cab proprietor, of Baker Street, Sparkhill.

8. The 'Golden Lion' Inn formerly stood in Deritend, a little nearer Birmingham and on the opposite side to the 'Old Crown' (below). Built about 1600, it was moved to Cannon Hill Park in 1911. This photographic card was published by Adams & Co. of Bristol Street.

9. Though the 'Old Crown' was built in 1368, it was considerably altered in the 16th century. Originally a manor house, it was later split into several dwellings before becoming a licensed premises. Card posted from Albrighton in November 1905.

10. Arthur Polton was the licensee at 84 Cambridge Street, Birmingham. Best Beer was 1d, Holt Championship Ale 1½d a glass. The Holt Brewery was in Holt Street, Aston. No indication of who published this postcard.

GT. WESTERN HOTEL & RAILWAY STN. ACOCKS GREEN.

11. The 'Great Western' Hotel, Yardley Road, was listed as a public house, not a hotel, in 1908. It has been rebuilt this century. The card was published by George Birch, newsagent, of Warwick Road, Acocks Green.

12. The 'Dolphin' Inn on the corner of Warwick Road and Green Lane (later Dolphin Lane, after the pub). It was later rebuilt and greatly enlarged, but demolished in 1992 to be replaced by a supermarket. Another card by local Acocks Green publisher George Birch, posted from Birmingham in May 1909.

13. Matthew Bissell was the licensee at the 'Spread Eagle' on the left of this view looking towards Acocks Green village from Victoria Road. It appears to have been demolished in the early 1920s. The card was published by H.P. Cartwright of Acocks Green and posted from there in November 1904.

14. The 'Barton's Arms' at Aston is a fine example of Victorian architecture, now restored. It is found at the corner of High Street and what used to be Potters Hill. Leonard, Smith & Co. of Cannon Street, Birmingham, published this card as no.6 in the 'Lens' series. It was mailed from the city in February 1906.

15. Scott Russell & Co. postcard featuring the 'Barton's Arms', with postal usage in October 1905. The surrounding houses and shops have been demolished and the area re-developed beyond recognition.

16. The 'Waggon & Horses' on the corner of Webster Street and High Street, Aston. An Ansells pub, it was listed in the early years of this century in Kelly's Directory under 'beer retailers' rather than 'public houses'.

17. The 'Junction' Inn at 224 Great Francis Street and 2 Bloomsbury Street sold Bullers' Wolverhampton Ales. Licensee in 1908 was John Simpson.

No 6   ALUM ROCK ROAD. BIRMINGHAM (2)

18. The 'Pelham' at the end of Alum Rock Road, featured here on this card by Heighway, posted in July 1929, was a Mitchells and Butlers House.

19. C. Markey's on the corner of Camp Street and Garrison Lane were bakers at the time this postcard was published. Earlier, however, they were beer retailers, selling A. Hood & Sons Ales. This brewery was at 30 Thimble Mill Lane, going out of business around 1900.

20. In the early years of this century, the 'Plough & Harrow' Hotel, Hagley Road, Edgbaston, was only listed as a public house, but was soon appearing as a Hotel. This may have coincided with the owner converting it into a limited company.

21. The 'Beggars Bush' was near the junction of Chester and Jockey Roads, Erdington. George Harding was the licensee at the time of this 1908 photograph.

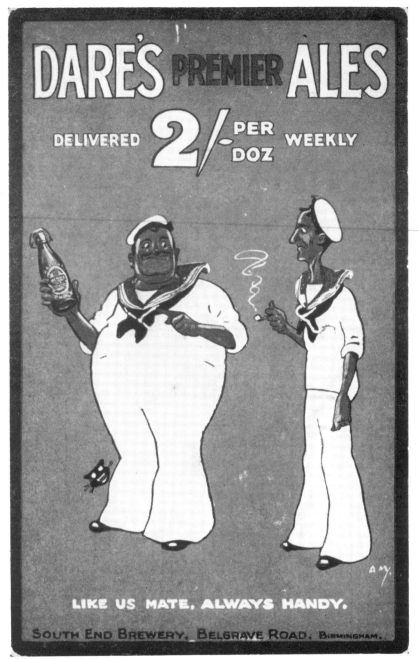

22. W. Dare's South End Brewery, Belgrave Road, was between Gooch Street and Frank Street. This advertising card would be left with customers for them to order supplies when necessary. The quoted price on the front (2/- per dozen) was, according to a rubber-stamped message on the back of the card *"subject to increased prices due to war tax."* Postcard designed and printed by David Allen & Sons Ltd of John Bright Street, Birmingham.

23. The 'Bulls Head' at Hall Green, now on the corner of Stratford and Fox Hollies Roads. It appears that there was a road or passage to the left of the pub for a sign there reads 'road closed'. Anonymously-published pre-1918 card.

24. The 'Horse Shoes', Stratford Road, Hall Green, just past School Road on the way to Shirley. The cart outside has on its tailboard *"G. Smith & Son, monumental sculptor, Sutton Coldfield."*

Highfield Road, Hall Green.

25. The 'Sherwood' public house, built in the 1930s on the corner of Highfield and Cole Valley Roads, Hall Green.

2721. ERDINGTON. AN OLD INN.

26. 'Ye Olde Green Man' at Erdington originated in the 15th century and when this postcard was published by R. Benton sold ale from Rushton's brewery at 69 Aston Road North and Chester Street.

27. The 'New Inns' at Handsworth on a card posted from Birmingham in August 1911. Selling Mitchells & Butlers ales, it was situated on the corner of Holyhead and Sandwell Roads.

28. The 'Villa Cross' at the junction of Lozells and Heathfield Roads. It sold Holt Brewery (from Aston) Pure Malt Ales.

Handsworth   Rookery   Road   Ana   Series   122

29. "Ana" series card no. 122 featuring the 'Farcroft' Hotel on the corner of Rookery and Albion Roads, Handsworth, which was built in the early 1920s. This postcard was posted from Birmingham in September 1925.

30. 'Ye Olde House at Home', Lordswood Road, Harborne, near the junction of Gillhurst Lane. It was listed as a 'beer retailer' in directories early this century, and sold Rushton's Noted Ales.

31. The 'Stork' on the corner of Heathfield and Finch (c.1907) the licensee was T. Bushill, presumably the ge Ales. No indication of the postcard publisher.

s in Handsworth. At the time this card was published
an in the centre. The pub sold Butler's Wolverhampton

32. The 'Junction' Hotel, straddling High Street and Vivian Road, Harborne. Mitchells & Butlers were the brewers.

33. The 'Woodman' Inn on the corner of Wells and Great Hampton Streets in Hockley, selling Holders Ales and Stout in 1911. The licensee, Mr. H. Wilson, and his daughter, here seen outside, were also at one time at the 'Plume of Feathers' in Shirley.

34. The 'Trafalgar' Hotel on the corner of Trafalgar and Woodbridge Roads, Moseley. This card was posted in August 1913 when H.C. Dentith was the licensee.

35. The 'Bulls Head' in Moseley village, which sold Burton's Ales in 1919 when this postcard was sent to Tunbridge Wells. On the right are the Mews, where J. Miles were cab proprietors. At the time there were, amazingly, 25 small firms connected with the gun trade in St. Mary's Row.

36. The 'Fighting Cocks' in Moseley village, on the corner of King Edward Road, was built between 1899 and 1903. Cock-fighting was held in the original tavern in the 18th century.

37. The 'Great Stone Inn', Church Road, Northfield, a Mitchells & Butlers House, and built in the 18th century. The village pound, to the left of the pub, held stray animals and was built of sandstone. This card was published by J.J. Davis, furniture dealer and fancy draper, at 120 and 130 Bristol Road, Northfield.

38. The 'Bull' Inn (licensee Hart Pilling), pictured in 1908 on a card published by Edwards & Co, New Street, Birmingham, in their "Clarence" series. The pub was on Bristol Road, Northfield, at its junction with Bell Lane.

39. The 'Boar's Head', Aldridge Road, Perry Barr, held by Ansells. Postcard published by Frank Nightingale in 1913.

40. The 'Church Tavern', Perry Barr, on a card published by Geo. E. Lewis, 62 Station Street, Birmingham, c.1907.

41. The 'Scott Arms' (right) on Walsall Road at Great Barr on a postcard sent from Hamstead in July 1916. Elsie wrote to Emmie: *"I am sending you the Scotts Arms. We have passed it but have not been in — rotten luck don't you think?"*

QN 21   THE STAG AND HORSESHOES. QUINTON   A TUCK CARD

42. The 'Stag and Horseshoes' at Quinton, a Mitchells and Butlers property. Raphael Tuck published the card, which was posted in May 1960.

43. The 'Gate Inn', 36 High Street, Saltley. The photograph appears to have been taken about 1860 before the Victorian development had taken place, but it was published as a postcard over four decades later by Isaac Squires, a photographer at 7 Bordesley Green Road. This card was posted in November 1907.

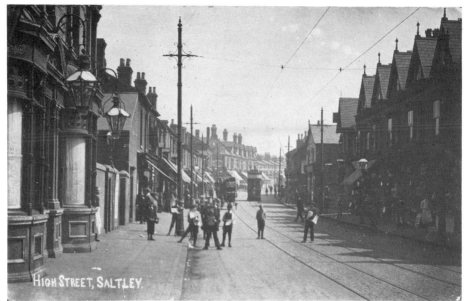

44. On the left is the frontage of the 'Adderley Arms' at 6 High Street, Saltley, when Jesse Stokes was the licensee. Postcard by unidentified photographer, posted in March 1910. The sender wanted to know if *"my dear S"* had got the craze for rinking yet.

45. The 'Angel' was a Georgian inn on the corner of Ladypool Road and Stratford Road. The square tower is that of St. Agatha's Church. Valentine of Dundee published the card, which was posted from Edgbaston in December 1904.

STRATFORD ROAD, (SHOWING NEW MERMAID), 1097.

46. The 'Mermaid Inn' at the junction of Warwick and Stratford Roads on a 1920s postcard, though taken from a much earlier photograph.

47. This photograph by Thos. Lewis shows the rebuilt 'Mermaid' (centre of picture) in the early part of this century. It has since been altered again, and at the time of publication of this book is closed and boarded up.

THE OLD OAK
SELLY OAK

48. The 'Oak Inn' on the corner of Harborne Lane and Bristol Road, Selly Oak, tooks its name from the tree in the foreground, felled in 1909. The inn followed nearly eighty years later, when it was demolished for redevelopment. The card was sent from Selly Oak in January 1912: *"I arrived home quite safe after a nasty journey stopping all the way"*. Cousin Dorothy had come back from Sutton Coldfield which would have taken 37 minutes, plus any time spent waiting for a connection at Birmingham New Street.

49. The 'Gun Barrels' on Bristol Road, near the junction with Edgbaston Road. A large number of public houses had a bowling green adjoining, but unfortunately most have ended up as car parks or building sites. A 1907 postcard, sent from Kings Heath in May of that year.

50. The 'Plough & Harrow' on the corner of Chapel Lane and High Street, Selly Oak, was known as the 'New Inn' until 1904. It sold Holt Ales. Across the road at no. 211, with a box-like frontage, was Walter Lilley, beer retailer, selling Butler's Ales. July 1905 postal usage from Selly Oak.

The Old Ship Inn, 1868.

51. The 'Ship Inn' at Camp Hill, established in 1560 and said to have been the head-quarters of Prince Rupert during his attack on the town in the Civil War. The old 'Ship', seen here on a 1904 card using an 1868 photograph, had pleasure gardens at the rear and sold Burtons Ales. It was formerly known as the 'Anchor'.

52. The old building was demolished towards the end of the last century and the Victorian structure seen on the right of this Thos. Lewis postcard took its place as the 'Ship Hotel'. This in its turn was demolished a decade ago for road improvements.

53. The 'Dogpool Inn' on the corner of Dogpool Lane and Pershore Road at Ten Acres, looking here towards Birmingham. On the diagonally opposite corner was the 'Ten Acres Tavern' *(see below)*. Both Inn and Tavern were demolished, and one new public house was rebuilt on the site of the Tavern, but renamed the 'Dogpool'. This card was posted in Birmingham in June 1915.

54. The 'Ten Acres Tavern' on the corner of St. Stephens Road and Pershore Road selling Holts Ales. Demolished and rebuilt as the 'Dogpool', it is now called the 'Hibernian'. Ten Acres Street Post Office is in the right foreground.

55. The 'Fox & Goose' at Washwood Heath Road, near the junction with Bromford Lane at Stechford, on a postcard published by the Midland View Co., Birmingham. In this 1908 card, 'home brewed ales' were advertised, along with 'good stabling'.

"FOX AND GOOSE" AND BROMFORD LANE, WARD END

56. The same pub after rebuilding in the thirties. The lane, the hedges and the trees have gone, replaced by an amazing collection of lamp standards and street signs. Postcard by A.R. Hill, stationer, Post Office, Coleshill Road, Ward End. It was sent from Birmingham in August 1937.

57. A view of the gardens at the rear of 'Ye Olde Barley Mow', St. Margarets Road, Ward End. Tom Bulluss was presumably the man featured, possibly the landlord.

58. The 'Waggon and Horses' on the Coventry Road at Lyndon End. The signpost directs travellers to Olton on the left and Marston Green Station on the right. The card was posted from South Yardley in August 1912.

59. The 'Swan Hotel' at Yardley, seen here on this 1910 postcard by J.P. Hughes of Small Heath, had a number of rebuildings in its history. The one shown here was replaced by what was claimed to be the largest public house in Europe. It was unsuccessful and closed down.

60. At the time when most of the postcards shown in this book were published (1904-12), delivery of ale and spirits was by horse-drawn vehicles, which of necessity limited the area of distribution. The advent of motorised vehicles — like this one belonging to Mackie and Gladstone, wholesalers, of 88-91 Dale End — spelt the death-knell of home brewing and small breweries.

61. The 'Travellers Rest' at Northfield, as it was originally built with a very unsuitable thatched roof, soon replaced with a tiled one. Mitchells & Butlers published this card themselves as a promotional item in connection with their Jubilee celebrations in 1929.

62. Another card in the same series, featuring the 'Beeches' at Northfield. Some copies of Mitchells & Butlers' book *"Fifty years of Brewing"* contained an envelope containing six postcards. The other four were *Cape Hill Brewery* (coloured), *'King George V' at Northfield, No.2 Brewery, Cape Hill,* and *one of the Malting Floors at Cape Hill.*

63. A later card by M. & B. with the slogan 'Good Honest Beer' on the reverse. This is the 'Stockland Inn' at Erdington.

64. From the same series: the Banqueting Rooms and Ball Room at 'New Inns Hotel', Holyhead Road, Handsworth. At least one other card exists in this series — *Hops in transit from the cold store to the brewery.*